T0013212

PRETEND YOU'RE IN PARIS

ALICE OEHR

Harper *by* Design

Bienvenue

To visit a new city is always an exciting and transformative experience, but there's no question that Paris has a little extra *je ne sais quoi*.

The clichés about Paris exist for a reason. Every street holds the promise of some life-changing sensory experience. Grand boulevards and small cobbled laneways reflect centuries of history, visible in every art nouveau metro station or retired palace you might pass. The sights and smells of the local cuisine inspire a kind of appetite you never knew you had. Perfectly coiffed poodles stroll elegantly beside their owners and even join them for lunch. Whether it's underground on the metro or admiring the view from on high at the Sacré-Cœur, the *joie de vivre* of Paris is all around.

As tourists, we are receptive to every moment – even the most everyday things seem spectacular. Having spent hours and serious money to reach our destination, we become determined to live each day to the fullest as we taste, see, feel and do as much as humanly possible in our limited time. We are the best version of ourselves when we relax, pay attention and make an effort. We are rewarded for years to come with our memories of all the places we visit.

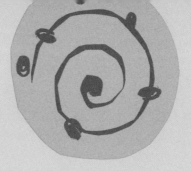

So how do we channel these curious and enthusiastic versions of ourselves into life at home? The end of a holiday shouldn't have to signal a return to our monotonous and stressful lives. Rather than simply rushing about from A to B, waiting for the sweet promise of our next vacation, we can start waking up to the pleasures and surprises of our own home towns. Paris is a fabulous city, sure – maybe the most fabulous in the world – but its real magic is reminding its millions of annual visitors how to feel alive. We find pleasure in new flavours, walking new routes, experiencing art and meeting new people. These things aren't exclusive to Paris at all.

Perhaps throughout this book, you might discover that many things we enjoy while holidaying can be found or created at home. Get up early and visit a new bakery or traipse across town to see how the light passes through the windows of an old cathedral. Take an aimless train ride just to gaze out at the passing countryside. Pay a visit to an exhibition at a local art gallery – big or small – then have an afternoon drink and toast to nothing in particular. You might just find that carefree feeling of Paris can be found close to home, after all.

How to use this book

Activating 'tourist mode' at home is easier in theory than in practice. It can be hard to get excited about the places where we conduct our daily lives – we think we know everything there is to know. But the more you look, the more you see.

This book has 50 DIY activities to channel the feeling of visiting Paris. They are split into five broad categories in no particular order, with several 'Paris at a glance' sections to give you a little extra context.

Food & Drink has you covered for meals – whether you're eating in or out – with enough French gusto to inspire a toast or two. **Architecture** encourages you to rediscover the details of your city, unveiling the history of the streets and squares right beneath your nose. **Art & Culture** invites you to re-examine the world through the eyes of others and even dress up to enjoy a night on the town. **Outdoors** has ideas for picnics, promenades and active ways of taking in the fresh air. **Fashion & Design** shares some secrets for dressing yourself (and your home) in the tradition of French fashion royalty.

A few things to bear in mind when pretending you're in Paris:

- Schedule your DIY activity in advance, and stick to it. 'Me time' is just as important as anything in your calendar.

- Tourist mode is available anytime – but it takes conscious effort. Just be present and curious, like you're in a new place.

- Pay attention to what's around you. Responsibilities can wait for a couple of hours (or days), just as they would on holiday.

- Phones should be used for happy snaps only – no sneakily checking work emails.

- Treat yourself – you're on holiday, after all. A lunchtime Champagne reminds you of all that's good in this life.

- Watch some French films, cooking shows or play some Édith Piaf to help you really get in the mood.

- Keep an open mind to trying something new. French culture is about engaging with art that makes you pause and reflect.

- The best things in life are free! Stroll around town, sit in the park or rearrange your entire room. No entry fees are needed.

WORKS OF ART

1

Paris's Musée du Louvre is famed for its gargantuan collection. To see everything is an exhausting mission that would take days and to properly appreciate each piece might take a lifetime. Engrossed gallery-goers may be oblivious to the fact that the Louvre was once a regal palace. Today, it houses a vast collection of hundreds of thousands of *objets d'art*, including Leonardo da Vinci's *Mona Lisa*. Tourists make a beeline for this tiny portrait and ensure it's always engulfed by crowds. To behold the Mona Lisa is certainly worthwhile, but to ignore the Louvre's many other marvels would be a grave mistake.

DIY Revisiting a museum or art gallery close to home can be freeing. You lose the pressure to 'clock' every masterpiece in one trip, knowing you'll likely return. Each time you return to an artwork (or collection) you bring different life experiences. Often, the more you look the more you see. The experience of locking eyes with the *Mona Lisa* has captivated viewers for centuries, but perhaps there is a portrait hanging near you with which you'll find a powerful connection.

A BISTRO SOIRÉE

2

Restaurants, cafes, tea salons, wine bars, breweries, bistros – the distinction between eateries in France dictates everything from the opening hours and complexity of cuisine to the luxury of decor and the flamboyance of your waiter. Whether it's a casual bite or a deluxe degustation you're after, this is a country that takes every meal seriously. For a relaxed option, a favourite among tourists and locals alike is the *brasserie* or the bistro. Both serve simple French fare all day long, without the pomp of a set lunch or dinner sitting. Slow-cooked casseroles, grilled meat or fish and salad or vegetables will always be on the menu – with a glass of house *vin* or *bière* to accompany, naturally.

DIY A simple bistro meal is a fun and relaxed way to spend an evening, alone or in company. Seek out a chic pub or casual neighbourhood restaurant and plan an evening out with friends. With everyone ordering their own plate, you get an evening of fun without any fuss or fanfare.

LOOKING FOR SIGNS

3

There are a number of ways to move through Paris, but driving might be the dodgiest. Crashes on roundabouts – like the one looping around the Arc de Triomphe – are so common that some insurance companies won't cover them. Plus, if you manage to find a parking spot, you'll need to be wary of 'touch parking' (the city-wide game of bumper cars). There's a network of rentable bikes and electric scooters, but most people in Paris – tourist or local – get around on the metro. The subway connects the whole city below ground, with each station its own architectural delight. While you're down there, listening to buskers, deciphering adverts and people-watching become more enjoyable pastimes than staring at your phone.

DIY The metro's architecture and signage are famous art nouveau relics. Pay attention to similar design choices in your city. Does your own public transport system, or do the street signs, tell a story? Are they beloved by design nerds? Do they reflect an aesthetic choice from the time your home town was designed? Do they communicate effectively how to get from A to B?

TRASH & TREASURE

4 The French love for second-hand shopping runs deep. Someone who hunts for hidden vintage gems is a *chineur*, and their efforts are rewarded with rare pieces at bargain prices. There are different tiers of second-hand shopping in France, each with pros and cons. *Vide-greniers* (garage sale) re-home old things at rock-bottom prices and offer a social element for shoppers. Stallholders make chit-chat and share coffees, making some extra euros during their spring clean. Serious antiquing goes down at the *brocantes*. They're full of rare collectables with clear provenance. Flea markets have the best of both worlds, with a mix of junk and valuable pieces. You know what they say about trash and treasure!

DIY Whenever you're thrifting, it pays to always keep an eye out for classic vintage pieces for your wardrobe. Learn the basic fabrics. Pure cotton, wool and silk items last well, unless moths get to them. If you come across any designer pieces from Chanel, Yves Saint Laurent or Dior, do some quick research on your phone to find a fair price. With any true market seller, haggling is expected.

A GOOD IMPRESSION

5

One of the defining art movements of Paris was born, as so many are, from rebellion. Fed up with strict and stifling painting conventions, artists like Monet, Renoir and Cézanne created revolutionary impressions of their subjects. In an era that churned out still lifes, portraits and landscapes, impressionists depicted daily life in a new style. These artists captured the mood of their subjects, rather than strictly what they saw. Thick daubs of paint were applied to the canvas, with brushstrokes left visible. Dream-like images of an ocean rendered in pink, purple and orange strokes or a patchwork pond of water lilies, left Parisians of the 1860s in shock.

DIY The ethos of an impressionist can be liberating. Try your hand at a still life, portrait or landscape. Gather some paints (thick acrylics are good for their texture) or pencils. Squint at your subject and see which colours leap out. Render this with deliberate, thick blobs, rather than blending areas together. Think about clashing colours and harmonious colours to balance areas of calm and chaos on the page.

MONUMENTS & MARKERS

6

Paris is adorned with sculptural tributes to people, events and military battles. Tourists seek out these public artworks for their beauty and to reflect on the long and tumultuous history of the city. There's the Luxor Obelisk, the glass pyramid at the Louvre Palace, the spectacular Arc de Triomphe and Paris's most beloved sculpture, *la tour Eiffel*. Whether you've met it in miniature on a key chain, seen it in a thousand films or have yourself ascended its grand arches, the Eiffel Tower remains the dominant symbol of the city the world loves to love.

DIY Do you ever notice the architectural markers on the streets of your own city? Take a walk around and note the buildings, statues or landmarks that seem significant. When and why were these things constructed? What do they signify, and how does the public feel about them? Have their meanings evolved over time? Be it a statue or just a small plaque, stopping to appreciate and understand these monuments can strengthen your relationship with the place you call home.

Next time you're in Paris, spare a thought for the city's bakers, who are up all night folding pastry into thousands of layers and swaddling loaves in towels. While we might view baking as one specific skill, the French make an important distinction between those who bake bread (*boulangers*) and those who bake cakes (*pâtissiers*). A baker may specialise or do both. In France, the *boulanger* is a true artist. They're experts in flours, yeast, sourdough cultures, handling dough and managing hot ovens, churning out hundreds of loaves each day to meet the demands of a population that really loves their bread. A baguette traditionally accompanies every French meal. It's spread with jam and dipped in morning coffee for breakfast; layered with butter, cheese and ham for lunch; and torn up and used to carefully polish the plate after dinner. The baking industry is closely moderated by French law – stipulating ratios of ingredients, as well as size and price – to ensure the quality of each and every loaf.

DIY Locate a decent artisan baker in your own town and head in early, if you can, for the freshly baked aroma. Of course, the classic French choice for a loaf is the baguette, but you might be in the mood for something dark, or with nuts. Sandwiches in Paris are always slim – rather than slathered with sauces or stuffed with ingredients. French sandwiches allow the bread to shine. To prepare your own Parisian lunch, gather an assortment of savoury toppings, like cheese, ham, salami, tomatoes, a little mustard and a scraping of French butter. Use your hands; French bread is typically torn, not sliced.

7

THE DAILY
BREAD

Seeing how the other half live is endlessly fascinating. Paris has housed many emperors, kings and queens, and before their heads were chopped off, they all resided somewhere suitably grand. There are many fabulous open-house museums in Paris that place you as a voyeur in someone else's life. One of the fanciest is the Musée Nissim de Camondo. Built in 1911, and the former home of Count Camondo, the mansion's original splendour is perfectly maintained. Guests peruse its many rooms to gawk at grand paintings, lavish tapestries and crystal chandeliers. While it's outside of Paris, Versailles is the palace to end all palaces. It's worth the day trip, but if you want to stay in the city (and gaze upon some art at the same time) the Musée du Louvre should scratch your palatial itch. The museum occupies the Louvre Palace, which was a royal residence between the 14th and 18th centuries. The Musée des Arts Décoratifs occupies a particularly ornate wing of the palace, which provides a marble backdrop for its collection of decorative artefacts. This 'museum within an old house' model is used in castles and mansions all over Paris and allows us regular folk a little insight into a life of luxury.

DIY Research any houses, mansions, palaces or notable dwellings in your home town to see if you can take a tour. Most cities will have a handful of famous houses or at least some interesting examples of architecture. Historical homes – lavish or otherwise – can be instant time machines. If no one lets you take a tour, be a (respectful) admirer from the street and let your imagination run wild.

8
LIVING
LAVISHLY

Food & Drink

From the luxe and lofty haute cuisine right down to the humble baguette, the French can do no wrong when it's time to eat. Even their snails taste good.

In the Parisian kitchen, sophisticated flavours allow fresh produce to shine, while exquisite presentation (and a flair for the dramatic) turns dining into an experience. For all its matched wines and featherlight soufflés, French cuisine might seem intimidating at first glance. But most dishes are the elegant result of a few simple ingredients, expertly prepared: a crisp green salad with a grilled *rondelle* of goat cheese and a drizzle of honey; a fresh cut of fish, sautéed in butter and herbs; a bowl of raspberries with Chantilly cream. It's all about the art of refinement.

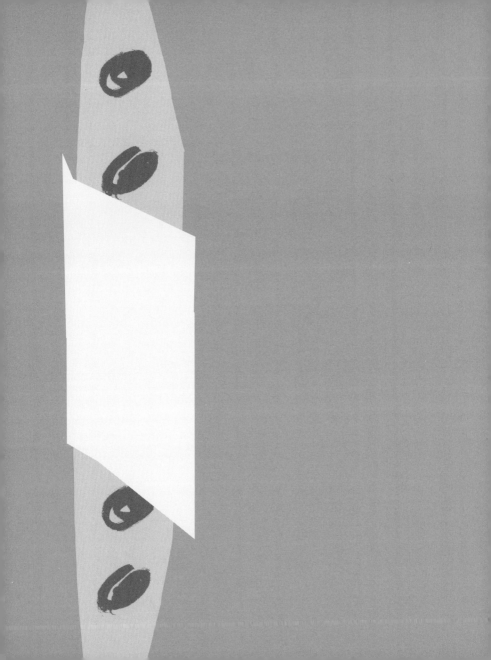

In Paris and across France, eating is a spiritual affair. Mealtimes are an important ritual, and every morsel is to be savoured with respect. Gone are the days when shops around the country shut between noon and 2 pm, so every French family could squeeze in a three-course meal and a siesta. But still today no self-respecting Parisian scoffs down lunch at their desk, or on the go. When it's time for lunch, even the most stressed executive in the city will sit down, take a pause and eat properly. That might be on a bench in the park, at a street-side table at a cafe, or perched upon the leather *banquette* of a *brasserie* (brewery). The lunch menu is often multi-course, providing a balance of tastes and textures, with a dash of adventure. Wine is always chosen carefully to enhance flavours and is consumed often, though rarely to excess. It's perfectly acceptable to have a glass at lunch.

BODIES OF WATER

9

Coursing through the centre of the city, *la Seine* splices Paris in half. The river provides an essential point of navigation in the city, as many of its iconic buildings and monuments are dotted along the banks. Historically, the *Rive Droite* (Right Bank) was occupied by the Parisian upper class, evident in opulent building facades and sweeping streets like the Champs-Élysées. The *Rive Gauche* (Left Bank) is known as the creative and bohemian heart of the city, where artists, musicians and philosophers have lived and created. These days, the Seine becomes a makeshift beach each summer. White sand is dumped at one or two points along the river, and umbrellas and deckchairs are laid out for sunbathers. Sipping an apéritif at Canal Saint-Martin on a summer evening, you can feel the electric atmosphere. Young, chic Parisians sit by this small section of the Seine to unwind with a drink and shake off the day.

DIY Is there a river, lake or canal in your city that you could visit? Take a boat ride, admire the view from a bridge, or swing your legs over the water's edge with a drink in hand. Bring some snacks to feed the local ducks, too.

Taste is ever-evolving, whether for food, fashion, furniture, art or design. In Paris, all things ornamental are celebrated in the Musée des Arts Décoratifs, where you'll see everything from ceramics, furniture and printing, to cabinetry, millenery and metalwork. The taste of any era is defined by the psyche of its people, as designers, artists and craftspeople reflect how society feels and aspires to feel. An object might speak to aspirations of modernity, glamour, practicality or sophistication (and sometimes all of the above). At this museum, you can spend hours admiring chairs through the ages, as well as dining tables, jewellery, lamps and wallpaper designs from various design movements. One fun thing you'll notice in this museum is the over-the-top panache with which so many French objects are decorated. Designed to flaunt luxury and wealth, these objects are varying degrees of good taste. Even if you can't imagine yourself owning a tasselled, gilded armchair, these flashy pieces are a feast for the eyes.

DIY Do some research into a French design movement and host a dinner party in that style. Art nouveau, with its flair for flora, or art deco, with its order and geometry, are good places to start. Invite your friends over and ask them to dress up in that style. Think about table settings and decor. A piece of fabric, some ornaments, flowers and lighting can set the right mood. Think about the music and menu. Art deco spaces communicate a chic, organised order, so your dining table should involve some clean lines and bold geometric decorations. If you fancy the rococo 'more is more' aesthetic, then go for it. Make your space overflow with gold, flowers, birds, cherubs and luxurious velvets and silks.

10

L'ART DE
L'OBJET

Paris is the home of haute couture for a reason. For those who visit the city during fashion week, the experience will not disappoint. Glittering pieces on the catwalk create awe and magic, while ready-to-wear collections in fashion boutiques are where you'll find outfits that you can actually afford. Legacy houses like Chanel, Yves Saint Laurent and Dior coexist with up-and-coming designers of today. To browse both old and new world fashion, the best spots in Paris are along fancy streets like the Boulevard Saint-Germain-des-Prés, which is lined with luxury boutiques. There's also the city's famous *grands magasins* – beautiful, sprawling department stores. These are worth visiting for their architecture alone. Like many institutions around Paris, the department stores offer a very sophisticated shopping experience. The glamorous spaces are teeming with garments, knowledgeable staff and even fancy restaurants with city views. It never hurts to catch your breath (and maybe have a wine break) while shopping.

DIY It pays to consider fashion the way you might view precious works in a museum. Take a day to go shopping, but ignore the lure of the spending spree and treat the adventure as 'cultural curiosity'. Enter boutiques and view clothing as you would fine art. Notice the colours, cuts, combinations, fabrics and accessories. How have they been put together? Does this remind you of any other designs? What could you do to put your own signature on the look? Take inspiration from anything you adore. Use that energy to remix what's already in your wardrobe.

11
HAUTE
COUTURE

NIGHT LIFE

12

Along with its wine and cocktail bars, Paris is also known for its cabaret and nightclub scene. When it opened in 1889, housed in an old windmill, the boisterous Moulin Rouge hosted shows every night. Skirt-lifting cancan dances became emblematic of the club's champagne-fuelled debauchery. The Moulin Rouge might be a tourist trap these days, but there are many clubs in Paris to catch a show or live performance. Since the roaring twenties, Paris has maintained a thriving jazz scene. American musicians flocked to Paris, and to great success. Artists of colour found that, at least compared with their segregated home towns, French audiences were less (overtly) racist. Josephine Baker won the adoration of France with her fabulous voice and energetic dancing (not to mention her iconic banana skirt).

DIY What does a night on the town look like in your city? Do you enjoy dancing, watching a performance or having a few nice drinks at a bar? Live music or a show can be a great way to spend an evening with friends. Have a look what is on offer and go and paint the town red!

The pre-dinner drink is one of France's finest traditions. Designed to stimulate the appetite before dinner, an apéritif also provides a ceremonial conclusion to the day. It's an opportunity to relax, unwind and let the evening commence. *L'apéro* is a very popular time to meet a friend – catch up over a drink, have a gossip, people-watch and just bask in the Parisian ambiance. Whether taken at home, in a picnic spot or at a classic Paris cafe, the general idea is the same: a drink (traditionally alcoholic) is served with a few savoury snacks to get you warmed up for dinner. Classic Parisian cafes and bars overflow each evening with people having knock-offs, as do all the parks and banks of the Seine in the warmer months.

DIY When choosing an *apéro* tipple, tradition dictates something more dry than sweet (save those for after dinner, to aid digestion). Beer, champagne, rosé or white wine all hit the spot, and travel well for a picnic. If you have access to a kitchen, go all out with a cocktail. A Kir Royale looks and sounds fancy, but is just champagne elevated with a dash of crème de cassis. French spirits are also worth a try, either over ice or mixed into a spritz. Look for the bitter Suze, sweet and sour Lillet or aniseed pastis. For gourmet snacks, make do with what's available locally. Chips, pretzels or olives are perfect if you're grabbing something en route to the park. If you have some time, consider crudités and dips or dainty things, like mini toasts with pâté, goat cheese with tomatoes, or tapenade and a bowl of cornichons. Put on some music, choose a nice spot and toast *santé* to shake off the day.

13
APÉRO
TIME

At one stage, Paris had the largest Roman Catholic population in the world. Many of its iconic churches reflect this past, although modern-day Paris is also home to many synagogues, temples and mosques. No sacred place has captured French imaginations like Notre-Dame. A spectacular example of French Gothic architecture, this building stands tall in the middle of the Seine on the Île de la Cité, adorned with a glorious rose window and hundreds of stone gargoyles. Immortalised in Victor Hugo's novel about a certain hunchbacked resident, the church saw a resurgence in popularity and a partial restoration following the publication of the book. In 2019, the world watched in horror as the cathedral burned. Fortunately, renovations and repairs are well underway, and Notre-Dame will stand strong *encore*. Sacré-Cœur Basilica sits atop the Montmartre neighbourhood, at the highest point in Paris. This beautiful white domed building is constructed entirely of travertine stone and shines down over every inch of of the city. The Sacré-Cœur celebrates French nationalist pride in subtle ways – the facade is framed by statues of Joan of Arc and Louis IX, while the giant bell hanging in the tower celebrates the attachment of Savoy to France in 1860.

DIY It's always worth checking out sacred spaces wherever you go, regardless of your beliefs. Whatever the era or religion, sacred spaces all over the world hold some of the most magnificent artworks and architectural feats made by humankind. Plan a visit to temples, mosques and churches near your own home. Think about these sacred spaces. In what styles are they built? How have they been decorated? Do they have modest facades with splendid interiors, or vice versa? How has the feeling of grandeur been heightened by the design and decoration?

14
SACRED
SPACES

URBAN GREENERY

15

Green spaces are more essential to our well-being than ever before. With increasing time spent indoors on screens, and holed up in high-rises, everyone needs regular fresh air and a stroll through greenery. Fortunately, nature is integral to the design of Paris. Glorious gardens have long been catwalks for locals to parade their latest fashions. Haussmann's renovation of Paris introduced lush places of reprieve from the busy boulevards, and new green spaces still crop up today. The Coulée Verte is a reclaimed above-ground railway line that has been planted into a 3.5-kilometre garden. The *promenade plantée (*planted walk), as it's known, offers a track with many shady spots for rest along the way. It was the first of many railway rejuvenations around the world, inspiring projects like New York's iconic High Line.

DIY Weather permitting, leave the office or home every day to take an outdoor break. Just 15 minutes spent reading a book or eating your lunch outside can be restorative. Make this screen-free time, if possible. Before putting your phone away, check the map for any nearby snippets of green space you've yet to explore.

EVERYDAY ELEGANCE

16

True Parisian style doesn't involve buying a new wardrobe every season. French approach favours refinement and simplicity. The 'less is more' maxim applies year-round, even when getting dolled up for a night on the town. The aesthetic is classic and timeless, with the occasional nod to passing trends. People consider clothing an investment, like buying fine art or sturdy furniture. The idea is that a new piece will complement what's already in your wardrobe and help you serve looks for many years to come.

DIY Try your hand at dressing French for a day and see how it makes you feel. This doesn't involve a striped top or jaunty beret. You don't need anything new at all; just dress with purpose. Coco Chanel famously advised that everyone, when getting dressed, should take one thing off before leaving the house. Less is always more. Respect quality materials and favour tailored cuts. Classic blue denim, a crisp white shirt or a good quality jacket – with a strand of beads, a hat or sharp tie – is a foolproof recipe for Parisian chic.

Architecture

So much of Paris's allure comes from the streets themselves. History and modernity are in harmony, as the patina of age meets cutting-edge design.

Famed for its verdant gardens, countless architectural masterpieces and unique layout, Paris is beautiful because it contains multitudes. Grand boulevards and public squares give way to winding cobblestone alleys of yesteryear. Cramped attic apartments offer views of giant gilded palaces and museums. Aggressively modern designs, like that of the Centre Pompidou, stand a short walk away from ancient Gothic cathedrals. This medley of styles, side-by-side, is one of the most captivating features of the city.

The snail shape of the *arrondissements* (neighbourhoods) in Paris is split in half by the Seine, which is criss-crossed by a number of grand bridges. The sense of symmetry and order that dictates the city centre came by order of Emperor Napoleon III, from the visionary mind of Baron Haussmann. Central buildings stand in tranquil uniformity – constructed to a standard height and style, in the creamy 'Paris stone'. The rhythmic pattern of these buildings is punctuated by statues, parks and historical monuments. Contemporary Paris lives in perfect balance with centuries of architectural history. Everyday retailers, like banks or supermarkets, find their homes in beautiful and awe-inspiring structures.

SMALL SPACES

17

Though notorious for loose plumbing, hundreds of stairs (maybe a rickety elevator, if you're lucky) and rodent problems, the classic Parisian apartment is a thing of beauty. The most recognisable is the Haussmannian style: a grand limestone building with a tin roof, internal courtyard, tall shutters and tiny wrought-iron balconies for the top floor. Elegant interiors might feature soaring windows, beautiful parquet floors and very high ceilings. It's the perfect backdrop for living the Parisian dream. Though some apartments are gigantic, the majority are modest. Artful details – like cushions, greenery, stacks of books, flowers and lamps – can disguise the fact that the bed is in the kitchen. Many apartments have small balconies that Parisians decorate with great flair to create oases of calm in these tiny spaces.

DIY Make the most of a small space by adding pot plants, lamps and cushions ... sometimes all you need is to rearrange your existing stuff. Find a space you could see yourself sitting and reading, or listening to music – somewhere near a window, perhaps – and set up your own cosy space there.

SWEET TREATS

18

Parisian *pâtisseries* display their cakes with love and attention, presenting them as a cabinet of jewels. For centuries their pastries have been celebrated around the world as works of art. Expert *pâtissiers* captured the hearts of French audiences long before the dawn of television and the celebrity chef. Some of their classic creations, like the mille-feuille, éclair and opera cake, look too perfect to eat (though most people manage). While tradition continues to play a significant role at the *pâtisserie*, there's room for innovation. Chefs that push the envelope might remix a classic with a new flavour (yuzu, pumpkin, pandan, sesame) or decorate creatively. In the Instagram age, any cake with a certain visual *je ne sais quoi* is a business asset.

DIY A slightly fancier kind of cafe, the local salon de thé is where Parisians might drink tea and enjoy macarons in the middle of the afternoon. To create your own afternoon tea at home, all you'll need is a nice tablecloth, a delicate cake purchased or baked for the occasion, and a pot of tea (French Earl Grey is a great choice) to wash it all down.

NICHE INTERESTS

19

Paris is packed with small museums that showcase everything about certain industries, people, processes or objects. Whether it's stamp-collecting, perfume-making or Édith Piaf, there's always something weird and wonderful to learn. You'll likely meet an interesting and passionate mind behind the front desk, too. Even if you don't have a niche interest (yet!), this is a great way to learn about the history and development of the city. Plus, these museums stock the most bizarre and interesting souvenirs in Paris.

DIY Have you ever taken the time to investigate what your own city might be famous for? The museums and books chronicling your home town might lend insight. Is your home town famous for a particular industry or export? Did anyone famous call it home? Sometimes it's just fun to learn about something niche, but going down the research rabbit hole might also introduce you to like-minded people.

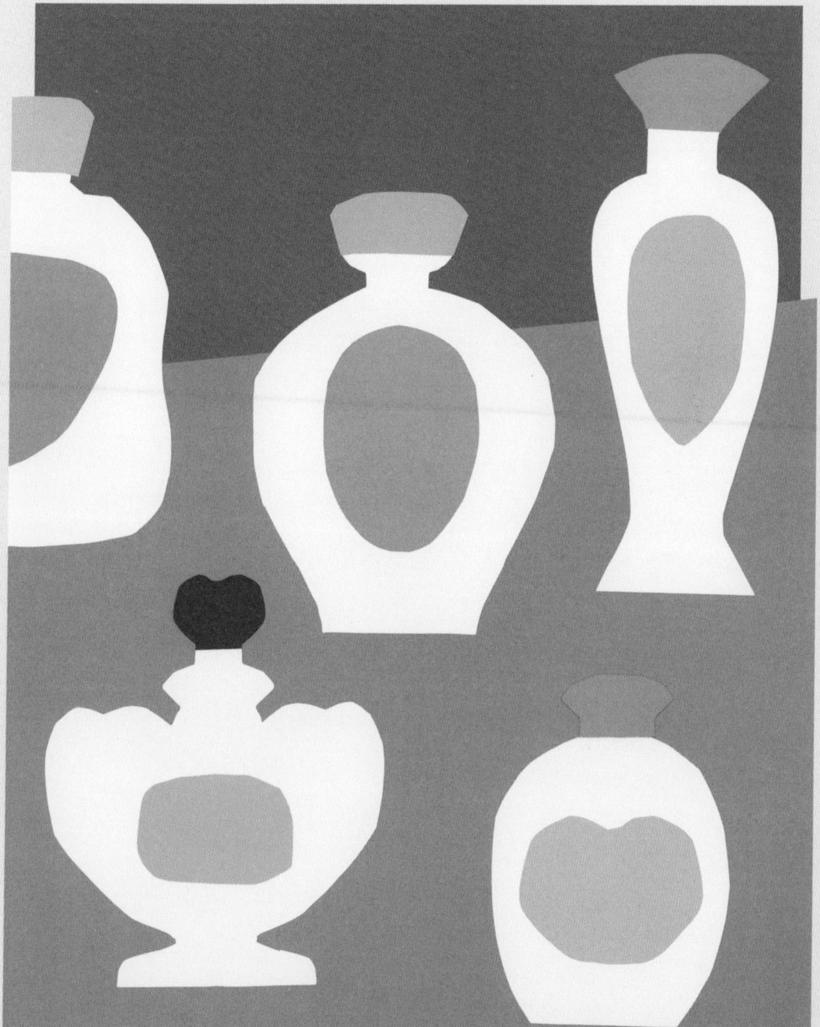

A LOVE THAT LASTS

20

The City of Light has inspired many grand gestures in the name of *amour*. There are daily proposals atop the Eiffel Tower, strolls down cobblestoned streets and picnic smooches on the grass by the Louvre. In recent years, one gesture has taken Paris by storm: inscribing a padlock with the names of you and your beloved, locking it to a bridge and tossing away the key. But love can be heavy sometimes. In 2015, over a million locks (weighing in at 45,000 tonnes) were removed from the Pont des Arts and lovingly re-homed to a wall nearby.

DIY Often the places of greatest personal significance to our lives are found close to home. Visiting these spots can connect us with our past and strengthen our sense of self in the present. Indulge your sentimental side and plan your own personal tribute to a certain time and place that you experienced a powerful moment of love. By yourself, or with a significant other, find a gesture to honour your memory. Plant a flower, take a photo or go with a padlock. Be imaginative and enjoy your trip down memory lane.

RITZY COCKTAILS

21

For the ultimate *oooh la la* ritzy Paris experience, you can't look past, well, the Ritz. Opened in 1898 by César Ritz, the iconic hotel was built behind an elegant facade overlooking the picturesque Place Vendôme. With impeccable service, lavish interiors and fine dining, the Ritz reinvented the entire hotel experience. Swanky amenities – like en suite bathrooms, electricity and telephones – were in every room. Only the most luxurious antiques and finest finishings decorated its halls. Needless to say, the Ritz was an instant success with its sophisticated clientele. The crème de la crème of Paris (and beyond) have visited the Ritz, from royals to politicians, actors to artists, and writers to singers. Still today, the Ritz upholds its reputation as one of the fanciest hotels in the world.

DIY Hop online and find the classic recipe for your favourite cocktail. For correct ratios, a shot glass should do the trick. Use either a cocktail shaker or large glass to mix. Ice is essential, as are some fancy garnishes – we're putting on the Ritz, after all. Go for olives, slices of lemon, twists of citrus peel, fresh berries. One Ritz classic is the Bloody Mary, especially for anyone drinking before noon.

THE
HIGH LIFE

22

The opera is always a grand affair, but to patronise Paris's Palais Garnier is another experience entirely. Commissioned by Emperor Napoleon III and breaking ground in 1861, architect Charles Garnier became the Opéra's namesake. Napoleon's taste was for anything blingy. Gold, marble, mirrors, statues, mosaics, velvet and crystal cover every inch. The Napoleon III style is an unconventional mishmash of design – baroque meets Renaissance, with a touch of ancient Greece – that shouts 'more is more'. Many buildings bedazzled at Napoleon's command stand proudly in Paris, each promising a fun and sparkling visit for all.

DIY Embrace the fanfare of the Opéra by staging your own glittering event. Book a movie, a play, a musical or cabaret evening. Invite friends and get totally dressed up. Make sure your evening includes all the trimmings: canapés, a cocktail or two, a fancy meal and perhaps some champagne. Doing this every once in a while makes for some unforgettable evenings.

SQUARES ARE HIP

23

When the Marais was chic the first time around, in the 17th century, it became home to Paris's first man-made square. The Place Royale (later renamed Place des Vosges) was commissioned by Henri IV as a large, central square, framed by four identical rows of perfectly symmetrical houses. Royals and nobility lived here, descending upon the square to catch up and host the odd jousting match or duel. Place des Vosges inspired similar designs around Europe and Paris. Across the city, these green oases help offset the bustling traffic. Nowadays, Place des Vosges is popular for picnics, apéritifs and walks. Archways along the perimeter host art galleries and restaurants, and some residences are open to visitors. Gravel pathways bisect stretches of manicured lawn, trees shade benches, and a beautiful fountain amuses kids and provides a romantic view for all.

DIY Perhaps your town has a nice green space you could enjoy? Plan a picnic there. Get fresh bread (a baguette, if possible) and a deli selection of cheeses, some ham or salami, pickles, olives and a small salad or two. Bring fruit, water and (need I say it?) wine.

France has more varieties of cheese than there are days in a year. Made from the milk of cows, sheep and goats, French cheeses are fermented to precise standards. The results come in all shapes, sizes and smells (from the young and fresh to the old and funky). Cheese is part of any balanced French diet, providing essential calcium, protein and umami deliciousness. In Paris, it's essential you visit the specialist *crémerie* (dairy shop) or *fromagerie* (cheesemonger). Many of these pungent shops employ an in-house *affineur* – an expert in the art of selecting and ripening cheeses – who can advise you on the best time to eat each variety. Like bread, there are standards for French cheese that mandate flavour, texture and appearance, before anything can be labelled as Camembert, cantal or Comté.

DIY When preparing your own cheese platter at home, there are some general rules about creating contrasts in flavour and texture. Offer something hard (Comté or Gruyère), something soft (Brie or Camembert), something goat or sheep and something blue. Aim for strong flavours, then some milder, fresher ones to balance them out. A variety of shapes and colours can make the board shine, too. Arrange the cheeses on a board with a couple of sharp knives and serve alongside fresh bread. A baguette, sourdough or rye breads make great accompaniments (the French would never use crackers). Lastly, when it comes to eating, warm up your palate with the mildest offering on the board (a young Camembert) and progress steadily to finish on the mature and strongly flavoured options, like a Roquefort.

24

FROMAGE

Outdoors

Picnics are the ultimate Parisian pastime. In the warmer months, the whole city seems to lounge around on the grass with a wine in hand. It's bliss.

Sunny days are rarely wasted by the French, and for anyone living in a small Parisian apartment, getting outside is an absolute necessity. Not all grass in Paris is for sitting, though. Many of the city's most famous gardens are treated as works of living art, and a 'look, don't touch' attitude is strictly enforced. Grand gardens frame and bolster the exterior of Paris's most fabulous buildings. The public can wander through these incredible topiaries, angular hedges and rows of flowerbeds. Ornate fountains, pagodas and statues please the eye and park benches provide the perfect place to catch your breath and while away the afternoon.

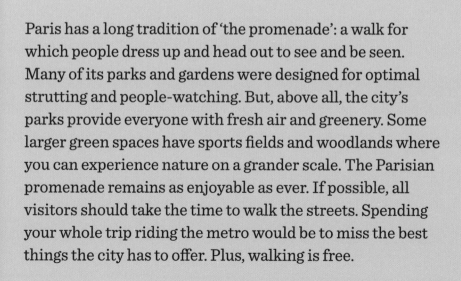

Paris has a long tradition of 'the promenade': a walk for which people dress up and head out to see and be seen. Many of its parks and gardens were designed for optimal strutting and people-watching. But, above all, the city's parks provide everyone with fresh air and greenery. Some larger green spaces have sports fields and woodlands where you can experience nature on a grander scale. The Parisian promenade remains as enjoyable as ever. If possible, all visitors should take the time to walk the streets. Spending your whole trip riding the metro would be to miss the best things the city has to offer. Plus, walking is free.

In the 18th and 19th centuries, noble men and women of Paris couldn't walk down the city's sewage-covered streets without dirtying their silk shoes. Rather than prioritising the waste problem, a network of arcades was built to aid the nobles' passage through the city. Hidden between parallel boulevards, these covered laneways became filled with shops so the aristocracy could do a little shopping on their shortcuts. Lined with marble floors and warmed by new gas lighting, these arcades provided the best way to cross town in style. Lined with tiny restaurants and shops, the passages serviced the tastes of those who visited. Luxury items were sold throughout: books, tailored goods, shoes, watches and jewellery. At one time there were more than 150 of these arcades, but today there are fewer than 20. In those that remain, you'll find shops that still specialise in things like vintage books, ephemera, clothing and toys.

DIY Maybe the design of your home town has shaped the way you and your community live, eat and shop. Are there hidden laneways that contain a goldmine of great shops? Is there a speakeasy you must be 'in the know' to enter? There are merits to being a local sometimes, especially when you're hosting friends or family from out of town, or if you're just fond of your own special spots.

25

HIDDEN
GEMS

BUILDINGS AS ART

26

Unsurprisingly, some of the most provocative art of the 20th century is housed in a museum with a controversial design. Constructed in the 1970s, the Centre Pompidou celebrates the materials and construction elements by making them design features. Plumbing, air conditioning and electrical wiring decorate the outside of the building, travelling in multicoloured pipes. Inside, collections include revolutionary movements like Fauvism, cubism, surrealism and Bauhaus. Like those upheavals of the art world, the Centre Pompidou's design is now celebrated by Parisians.

DIY Do some research into the buildings of your own city. Are there any conceptual pieces of architecture that provoked a strong reaction when they were built? Often anything left of field becomes controversial and evokes a love/hate response. See if there was a reason the architect chose that style. Find out if locals have warmed to it or if it remains unpopular today. Maybe visiting these places will feel different after learning about their context?

A GLASS HALF FULL

27

France (arguably) produces the finest selection of wines in the world. Most French people have a basic knowledge of when and how to best choose a glass. There are over 50 grape varieties grown across France, and every factor in the environment where they're grown is significant, from the soil composition to the sun, wind and rain. Like cheesemaking, French winemaking is an art form. While a true connoisseur can discern tiny subtleties between each bottle, the best place to start is by trying a few yourself and seeing what you like.

DIY Start by visiting a bottle shop and seeking advice. Be clear about what you enjoy and ask for pairing recommendations. As a general rule, white wines pair well with white meats whereas reds complement red meats. Champagne or sparkling wine is customary for celebrations. Fortified wines are often drunk as apéritifs, while sweet dessert wines usually come out for a post-feast tipple. The flavours of certain foods and drinks can benefit greatly from each other's company, so experiment for your next soirée.

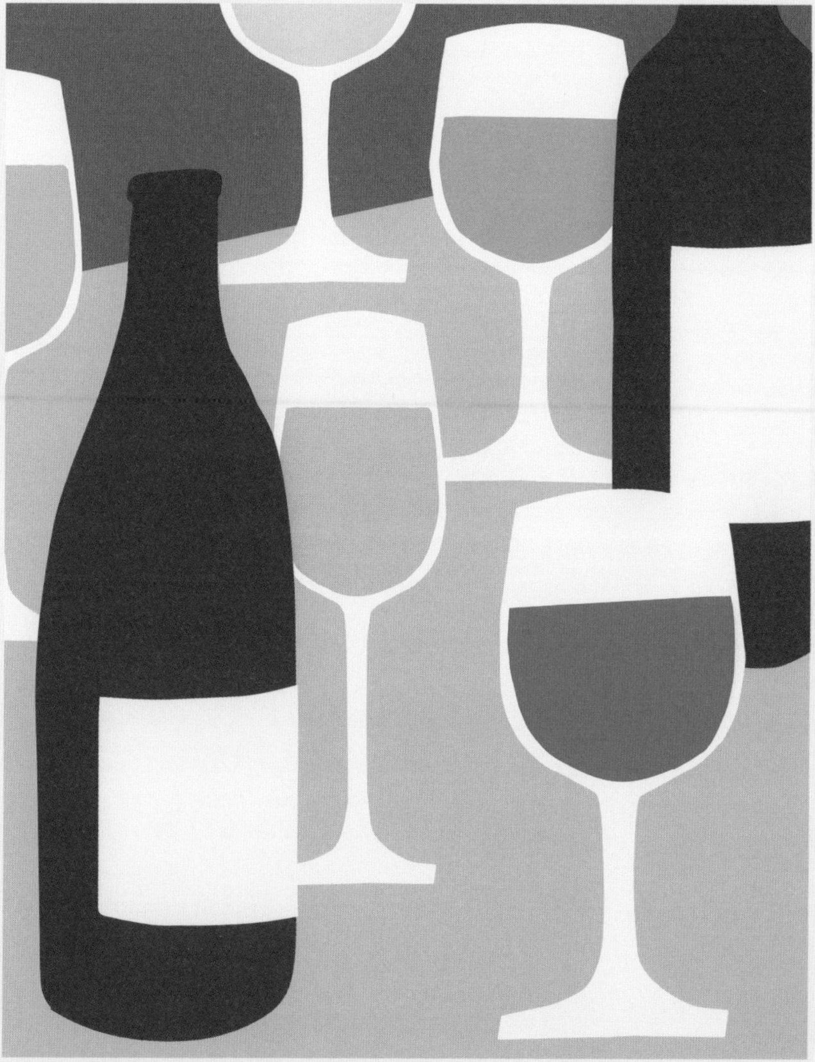

From any home in Paris, the seaside, ski slopes and countryside are just a train ride away. France's intricate railway system snakes across the country, providing a cheap, comfortable and accessible way for Parisians to take a *vacances*. Though we take it for granted today – with millions commuting on French trains each day – train travel was once a luxury for those who could afford to holiday to the Côte d'Azur, the Alps or further afield in Italy and Switzerland. The bygone grandeur of train travel can be found in the giant railway stations of France's biggest cities. Paris's Gare du Nord and Gare Montparnasse are cavernous glass structures, with spectacular restaurants below ground. Catching the train in France holds a certain romance for holidaymakers, made all the more entertaining at mealtimes. Nearly all passengers pack their own train picnic, and gourmet plates are available from the restaurant car. At midday and 7 pm, the fizz of drinks being opened can be heard in every carriage.

DIY Free from the stresses of airport security or the tedium of driving, taking a train trip – even just for a day – is a simple way to clear your head. Plus, trains usually allow you to bring dogs, surfboards and bikes. Look up train destinations in your area and plan a getaway for a day, weekend or week. Pack a train picnic. Grab some magazines or a crossword book. Download a new playlist. Spend some time looking out the window doing nothing. Catching rhythmic glimpses of passing landscapes is meditative. It's a great way to zone out and bring about a nap.

28
TRAVEL BY
TRAIN

SURREAL LIFE

29

In the free-thinking atmosphere of Belle Époque Paris, artists flocked to the bohemian neighbourhoods of Montmartre and Montparnasse. The nightlife was legendary, with revolutionary ideas fleshed out at cafe tables and clubs. From this milieu came the visual and conceptual style surrealism. Championed by Salvador Dalí, Andre Bréton and René Magritte (among others), the movement produced bizarre paintings, films, literature, music and theatre that questioned the bounds of reality and perception. Surrealists used Freud's theories on psychology, their own dreams and the absurd to juxtapose imagination with reality through imagery and ideas.

DIY To create a surrealist collage, grab a couple of old magazines. Cut them up then paste snippets down to form a whole new reality on the page. Create a background then add some characters or objects. Remix time and space to create an entirely new world. Reposition ordinary things side by side in a way that will confuse, amuse and challenge our notions of reality.

In Paris, there are nice gardens and then there are next-level *jardins*. The latter are elaborately manicured, professionally designed and tirelessly maintained. Many of Paris's famous gardens are palatial in scale, often literally framing a palace or château. The art form of designing gardens really took off in the 17th century. André Le Nôtre, who landscaped the vast Gardens of Versailles, was famed for his elaborate and artistic sceneries. His designs are replete with mazes, box hedges, exotic plants, manicured lawns, fountains and statues. For formal gardens in France, plants are moulded into obedience to create geometric designs and sculptures. Principles of symmetry and harmony provide a beautiful space to move through, as well as making châteaus look spectacular. When looking for a Parisian garden, you'll be spoiled for choice. The Luxembourg and the Tuileries gardens are, perhaps, the most well known, but all over Paris you'll find gardens buzzing with both locals and tourists. Garden-goers can be seen walking and talking, eating on benches, taking naps, playing boules, sailing a boat on the fountain and just admiring the view. Some gardens won't allow you to step on the grass. Should anyone miss the warning signs, wardens are quick to come and blow their whistle (and provide a terse lesson in etiquette).

DIY Most cities have a large park or two, and, if you're lucky, botanical gardens. Plan a visit to promenade around, play a game, take a break or sip a nice cool drink. Have a nap on the grass. Consider the landscape design. Are there dainty manicured beds, sweeping lawns or recurring visual themes? How have colour, shape and height been used? What plants can you identify, and where in the world do they come from? Does the flora yield to human intervention, or does it run wild and free?

30
GREAT
JARDINS

One of the most exciting things about travelling is learning the nuances of other cultures and their routines. A typical French breakfast (*petit déjeuner*) is simple and delicious. Plus, despite everything you've read about butter and the French, it's pretty healthy. Most Parisians start the day with a croissant, or toasted baguette spread with butter and jam, dipped in a small bowl of coffee. Kids might have a *chocolat chaud* (hot chocolate) and a piece of fruit, natural yoghurt or fried eggs. Remember, lunch is at midday and might involve multiple courses – and multiple wines – so save room. If you take your *petit déj* in a cafe, you can appreciate the ceremony from a street table while you watch Paris wake up. But if you happen to be busy and important, you can have a *petit café* (espresso) standing at the bar, skimming through *Le Monde* newspaper or chatting with the bartender, before moving on.

DIY To start your day the French way, you'll need a pastry and a hot drink served in a bowl. Hot chocolate or milky coffee is the norm. A day-old baguette might feel as hard as rock, but it's still great for toasting and spreading with jam. If you feel like venturing into the morning, choose a cafe with a great view of the street. Look out as you sip your coffee – your phone can wait. It's all about people-watching, having some banter with the waiter or another patron, and getting lost in your own thoughts as you prepare for the day. A croissant on the side never goes astray.

31
PETIT
DÉJEUNER

BOOK WORMS

32

Screens are seductive, but nothing compares to reading the good old-fashioned way. Bookshops in France celebrate the printed word, and are often filled with heaving shelves and stacks extending to the floor. Shakespeare and Company is a pilgrimage for all literature lovers. It has changed hands from father to daughter, all the while serving as a hub for ex-pat writers to meet their creative family between the shelves. In the 1920s, it was a hangout for F. Scott Fitzgerald, Gertrude Stein, James Joyce and Ernest Hemingway. Bookworms visiting Paris are drawn to the *bouquinistes* (small, second-hand booksellers) that border the Seine. Against this stunning backdrop you can hunt for second-hand books as well as artworks and souvenirs (plus the chance to pick up a rare early edition).

DIY Visit your local bookshop (the smaller the better, as these are usually curated by a passionate owner) and get lost in the shelves for a while. Examine the covers, read the blurbs and see what takes your fancy. Chat with the staff; they'll certainly be well read. Return home with a new title or two and treat yourself to a relaxing afternoon on the couch.

Art & Culture

Paris has been the artistic capital of the Western world for centuries - and with good reason! There are legions of galleries and museums to prove it.

Tourists don't have to pay admission to the Louvre to find the art in Paris. They need only walk down the street or pull up a seat at the bar. Painters, writers, singers, musicians – artists of all stripes – fill the city. They flock to its cafes and bars to swap ideas, collaborate and just generally have a good time. Bohemian neighbourhoods like Montmartre have long been a hub for artists from around France and the globe. Many visitors and residents of Paris have become household names and idols of the art world.

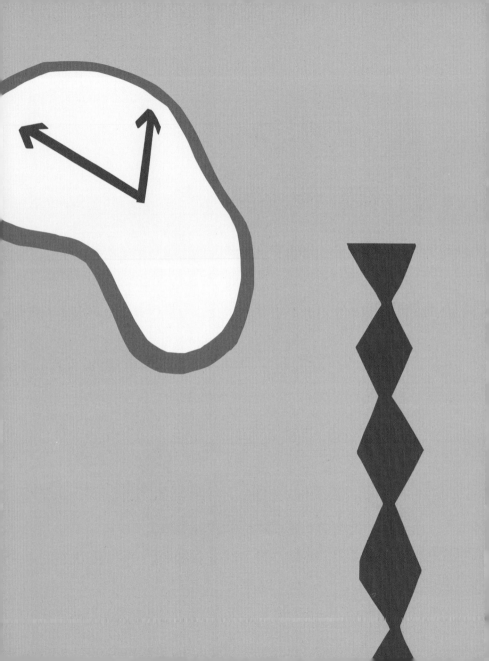

You'll never be short of cultural offerings in Paris. Locals and tourists converge to celebrate live music, theatre, film, opera and dance. French culture places an emphasis on curiosity and celebrates critical thought and discussion. Galleries and museums feature the works of 20th-century giants and emerging artists with the same enthusiasm. Major exhibitions stimulate discussion. Most importantly, art in Paris is not just for 'arty' people. It's common for anyone to catch an exhibition with a friend before retiring to the bar to discuss what they've seen. People from all walks of life enjoy the arts in Paris, and festivals like the *Fête de la Musique* (World Music Day) transform the entire city into a cultural playground.

POINT OF VIEW

33

Paris is built on undulating terrain, with plenty of hills worth conquering for their views. The bohemian Montmartre is just as famous for its picturesque streets as for the many colourful characters who make mischief there. Whether you snake up the backstreets or climb directly up the 234 steps to Sacré-Cœur, you will be rewarded with a sweeping view of the whole city below. Belleville is another stunning hilltop neighbourhood, where you can explore the Parc des Buttes Chaumont and feel you're entirely out of the city. If parks aren't your thing, take a lift or escalator to the top of the Pompidou Centre, Arc de Triomphe or the Galeries Lafayette department store to take in the spectacular (almost) bird's-eye view of Paris.

DIY Try to find an elevated lookout in your city (natural or man-made). Whether it's taking a lift to a rooftop, climbing hundreds of stairs or trekking up a mountain, it's always worth the effort. Look around and you'll feel humbled. Enjoy a world-class view over some of humankind's greatest accomplishments: architecture, engineering and community.

Previously a swamp, the Marais (literally, 'the marsh') became a hotspot for the Parisian aristocracy from the 13th to 17th centuries. After the French Revolution, the Marais lost its status with the nobility, and instead became a thriving hub for the Jewish community. Today, the Marais is back in vogue, and we can thank this Jewish influence for blessing the neighbourhood with some of the best eateries in Paris. Falafel shops and bakeries in the Marais draw massive crowds each day, and the entire area is always buzzing. There are trendy boutiques by young designers, a cosmopolitan mix of restaurants, relaxed pubs, riotous gay bars, lush parks and a dense concentration of small art galleries. The Marais is also home to the Musée Picasso, where you can see over 5,000 works by the co-founder of cubism.

DIY Find the spots in your city that attract young or up-and-coming designers, artists and artisans. There'll be a kind of electricity in the air. Wander through these artsy hubs and see what they have to offer. Grab some food and a cocktail. Do some window shopping and find something handmade. Pop into a boutique art gallery. Keep an open mind and, as always, allow yourself to be surprised.

34
C'EST
CHIC

REST IN PEACE

35

One of Paris's most popular tourist destinations is the Père Lachaise Cemetery. This leafy space is the largest of its kind in Paris, and the final resting place for many war heroes and artists. Adoring readers pay their respects to literary greats like Marcel Proust and Oscar Wilde, while musicians seek the graves of Jim Morrison and Édith Piaf. Visitors have honoured their heroes in some rather creative ways, so the graves are now closely monitored to keep the tributes tasteful. Meanwhile, on the other side of the city, an art nouveau cemetery celebrates the lives of hundreds of Parisian pets. Tombstones there honour departed furry, feathered and fishy friends.

DIY Strolling through a local cemetery (in the daytime, ideally) is a great opportunity to pause and reflect on your own life. Seeing the names of those who came before you can be enlightening. You might see some of your own ancestors, or a famous name or two. Most importantly, a visit to any cemetery serves as a reminder that we're only here for a short (hopefully good!) time, so we would be wise to make the most of it.

MARKET DAY

36

Even with supermarkets in every neighbourhood, street markets remain an integral part of the French way of life. Markets are where locals go to stock the fridge and get inspired. Many French homes only cook what's available at the market each day, enjoying every variety of fruit and vegetable by eating them at the height of their season when they have the most flavour. Savvy market-goers will ask stall holders when to expect green beans, apricots, cherries or truffles. In this way, going to the market is incredibly social. Grabbing groceries becomes a pleasure, where shoppers trade conversation, take in the fresh air and share plans for their baskets of produce.

DIY You may have to do a little research, but most cities have some type of farmer's market each weekend. These places often have an organic bent and offer the opportunity to purchase goods directly from the grower. Ask their advice for the best way to prepare and enjoy their produce. Make the market trip an entire morning affair. Don't rush. Ask questions and shop for fruit and vegetables that are in season, to prepare and enjoy meals for both lunch and dinner.

The summer solstice is marked in Paris with a city-wide celebration. A tradition since the 1980s, the annual *Fête de la Musique*, or World Music Day, sees musicians take to the streets. There are organised (and impromptu) performances in concert stadiums, bars, parks and even street corners and balconies. The longest day of the year guarantees a bright, hot night, and there's a palpable party atmosphere throughout the city. Musicians on World Music Day perform for free, taking their love of music and the joy it brings to the streets of Paris. Jazz is one of the most popular sounds throughout the festival, helping the city unite before everyone flees to the coast for the stifling French summer.

DIY Following France's example, 21 June is now celebrated everywhere as World Music Day, which is a great excuse for a party. Choose a theme and have your friends over to celebrate. Everyone might bring a favourite record or create a shared playlist. You could theme your fête around one genre of music. If anyone at your party can play an instrument or sing, ask them to play a little set. If you have fun neighbours, let the party spill out into the street and invite passers-by to join in.

37
STREET
MUSIQUE

STONE SOULS

38

Paris's many statues serve to both commemorate and inspire. The Place de la République houses a giant bronze Marianne – the personification of liberty, equality and fraternity – that's a meeting point for protests and social gatherings. The sculptures of Auguste Rodin, like *The Thinker* and *The Kiss*, capture individuals rather than an idea or a figure from mythology. As Rodin saw it, *The Thinker*'s tense posture spoke to human nature more than the smooth musculature of Greek gods and goddesses. Romanian-born Constantin Brâncuși also sculpted a piece called *The Kiss*. Using stone, wood and bronze, Brâncuși rendered familiar subjects (a feather, a fish, a face) in elegant geometric forms. Through these tactile objects, appearing light and forceful all at once, Brâncuși flexed the true power of stone.

DIY Do you have sculptures in your city that celebrate something, or express the view of an artist? Are they representational or abstract? What do they mean for your community, and how do people respond to them? Perhaps some rub the foot of the sculpture for good luck or lay flowers at its base.

WALK LIKE A PARISIAN

39

The best way to see Paris is *à pied* (on foot). The metro may be quick, but you'll miss the city's finest offerings: fabulous buildings, decorative shop signs, chic Parisians and their dogs, the wafting perfume of a bakery, waiters clashing with cafe customers, haute couture window displays ... The list goes on. The diversity of streets is extraordinary, from the broad boulevards of Saint-Germain-des-Prés to the narrow cobble-stoned hills of Montmartre. Paris's snail-like map of numbered *arrondissements* may seem confusing, but it makes sense eventually. Beginning on the Île de la Cité, the neighbourhoods spiral out from one to 19. If you ever get lost, just look for these numbers on any street sign.

DIY Set aside some time to plan an urban adventure in your own city, being sure to explore as much as possible on foot. Head to the centre of town and see the main drag or start with your own neighbourhood. Wander the streets as though you are a tourist. Take a new route and don't hurry. Notice the architecture, shop signs and street names, and how they fit together.

PAMPERED POOCHES

40

For the pooches of Paris, life is pretty sweet. If you're small and well-behaved, you'll be welcomed everywhere. For designer dogs, like a carefully coiffed poodle, there are plenty of pricey salons to get a blow-dry or mani-pedi. Accessories are kept to a minimum; for Parisians, diamanté collars and mini puffer vests are gauche distractions from a pup's natural beauty. While *chiens* can shop at Chanel and dine at Michelin-starred restaurants, Parisian pooches aren't allowed to run around city parks carte blanche. Fines are steep for owners who leave their dog's *crotte* (no comment) behind. Still, it's worth keeping an eye out for hazards.

DIY The joy dogs feel in a park is contagious. Going for a stroll with a canine friend – or sitting in the park to dog-watch – will always lift your spirits. In Paris, dedicated dog parks provide spaces for the dignified doggos to be ridiculous by chasing each other, rolling in the dirt and procuring sticks. If a friend or neighbour needs time off their canine duties, offer to take their dog to the park once a week.

Fashion & Design

If there's one thing to envy about Parisians, it's their chic sensibility. Everything's refined - from sleek restaurant decor to the cut of a coat on the catwalk.

Aesthetics have long been valued by the people of Paris. For centuries, the city's royalty and nobility set the standard for decor by throwing wealth behind the embellishment of their living quarters. As time went on, design trends began to reflect the ethos of people on the street. Modernity and its ideals are embodied by the Eiffel Tower. The clean lines of art deco, as well as the romance of art nouveau, define the city's many facades. Paris shows its visitors exemplars of great design from every era.

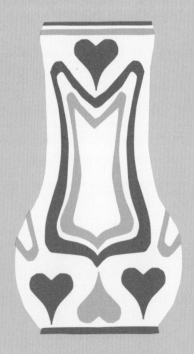

Fashion in Paris is known for being cutting-edge. When shopping, there are options to suit all budgets in the city's boutiques and department stores. The frills and fanfare of fashion week's catwalk are at odds with the taste of locals on the street. Streetwear in Paris is defined by a classic, understated elegance. As always, it comes down to being chic. This chicness transcends fashion – you'll find it in every corner of Paris. From the detailed facades of buildings to the manicured parks they overlook. You'll find it in the spirit of sweet old ladies sitting at cafe tables, with coiffed canine companions poking out of designer bags. It's easy to see in Paris, and you can even take it home with you.

With their marble-top tables and views of passers-by, the cafes of Paris serve the locals and capture the imaginations of tourists. Street seating allows patrons to see and be seen. Historically, these cafes have been the places artists, philosophers, writers, musicians and designers congregate. Revolutionaries would sip coffees and wine, discussing the ideas and politics of the day while basking in the atmosphere. Parisian apartments usually have tiny kitchens – if they have any kitchen at all – so locals visited *bouillons* (soup kitchens) and cafes for their daily feed. Alongside the conversation, coffee and booze, these French cafes offered sophisticated food, like steak frites. Even today, the cafes of Paris continue to host locals and tourists alike. They're a melting pot of the literati, glitterati and anyone looking for a moment of peace at a quiet corner table.

DIY The atmosphere of a Parisian cafe can easily be recreated closer to home. Take the pressure off whichever friend always hosts dinner parties by inviting everyone out for a drink. See if any local bars serve cocktails in the afternoon, or there might be a pub in your neighbourhood with a chic beer garden. If you really want to feel like a French philosopher, think of some tricky topics you'd like to chat about in advance. A night of fun will surely ensue.

41
CAFE
CULTURE

FINE DINING

42

In Paris, a *grand restaurant* is where you'll find the hallmarks of haute cuisine. Tailored to the rich tastes of French aristocracy, this style persists today for its mastery of complex culinary techniques (reductions, flambé) and lavish ingredients (truffle, foie gras). When dining at a *grand restaurant*, you can expect a luxurious classical interior and to be greeted by a suave maître d'hôtel. The full-course meal might begin with seasonal salads, small fish, charcuterie or pâté. Your *plat* (main) could be poultry, meat or fish, with seasonal vegetables or *jus*. Finally, there's cheeses, a green leafy salad and something sweet before a farewell coffee.

DIY Recreate a fancy French restaurant at home. Plan to make three courses that vary in flavour and texture. You should be guided by what's in season and prepare as much as possible in advance. For apéritif hour, set the scene with music, candles and soft lighting. Lay a tablecloth and even display a handwritten menu. Dress up and ask your guests to do the same. Serve drinks and snacks on arrival, then take your time to enjoy a long and lavish meal. Wrap up the evening with a tea, coffee or digestif.

RITUAL RELAXATION

43

Paris has long been a diverse and multicultural city, and the spectacular Grande Mosquée de Paris is a vital place of worship for its Muslim community. Inspired by a similar design in Morocco, the Parisian mosque has a grand minaret tower standing 33 metres high that is the largest in France. Its exterior is resplendent with blue and silver tiles, and inside the ceilings are tiled with exquisite mosaics laid by expert North African craftspeople. Within the grounds of the mosque there's a restaurant, tea room, shop, courtyard garden and traditional Turkish bathhouse. It's a popular destination for tourists wanting a moment of calm in beautiful surrounds.

DIY As well as a place to learn about Islam, the mosque in Paris is a spot for introspection. Making time for yourself is critical for your mental and physical well-being. Plan a quiet cup of tea, sit in the park or have a bath. Look away from the screen and zone out. Now, more than ever, the benefits of mindfulness and meditation are obvious. Any kind of regular me-time will always do you good.

EXPERT ADVICE

44

In Paris, and across France, the specialist shop is still revered. You'll find them run by humble experts all over the country. Small establishments devote themselves to niche goods, like spices, chocolate, fish, chicken, cheese and tea. These stores are the antithesis of the modern supermarket, and always worth the extra effort to visit. The French shop at specialist purveyors for both the quality of the goods and the wisdom of the proprietors. Zipping through the self-serve checkout is a poor substitute for chatting with an expert. Especially if you're hunting for the perfect truffle.

DIY Visit a specialist shop near you that's been in one family for generations. You might be surprised by what you find. The local butcher, fishmonger or small greengrocer is bound to be an expert on their fare – so, talk to them. Carve out some time to enjoy shopping and cooking for a special dinner. Be guided by what you stumble across rather than adhering to a shopping list or recipe. Try a new spice or sauce and keep an open mind when taking recommendations from the experts.

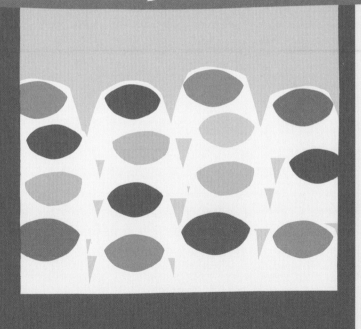

Many famous Parisian artists, like Pablo Picasso and Paul Gauguin, were influenced by the art of indigenous cultures in their work. They travelled to (and collected artefacts from) far-flung cultures, learning new approaches to style and storytelling. Picasso's cubist works – especially those which celebrated the imagery of African sculptures and masks – rebuked the realist oil paintings that dominated French galleries. Drawing freely in his sketches, Picasso could simplify subjects into blocky geometric forms and present a fresh perspective of a person or place. In his mission to reimagine – rather than merely replicate – reality, Picasso engaged with ideas and artmaking from many cultures. The results captivated audiences, and the incredibly high praise (and valuations) his work receives today is well deserved.

DIY Drawing freely is not as easy as it sounds. To prepare for his paintings, Picasso created elegant sketches using a single line or loose shape, with just a few details to convey his subject. Try this approach for yourself by shifting your focus from the final sketch to the journey of the drawing itself. Think of it like a 'telephone doodle', something you'd do without concentrating. Choose a subject (an apple, a person, a vase) and try drawing it in one or two lines, without lifting your pen. Remember, anything goes; your drawing can be whatever you say it is.

45

GEOMETRIC
LINES

PELOTON PARTY

46

The Tour de France is as much a cycling event as it is a national festival. Professional cyclists flock to France to compete in this gruelling 23-day race, riding through 21 stages (mini races) around the country. For over 3,500 kilometres, these athletes race on alpine and rural terrain, before a grand finish at the Arc de Triomphe. Millions of spectators compete, in their own way, for the best spots to cheer along the route. *Le Tour,* as it's affectionately known, has been a tradition for over 100 years. Despite repeat doping controversies, the race is wildly popular. Sadly, the tour remains boys only (though there are whispers of change). Nevertheless, cycling is popular around the country, with French hobbyists pedalling for exercise, to commute and when touring their fine country.

DIY Rustle up a peloton and plan your route for a wholesome weekend ride. Head away from the city traffic. Assign someone to be the navigator and put someone else in charge of the picnic. Ride for a few hours to a scenic spot where you can properly rest and refuel before the journey home. Support your fellow riders and remember that Lycra is absolutely optional.

In the realms of art and design, Paris respects its history and embraces progressiveness. Critical thinking and discussion are inherent to Parisian culture. Like the radical impressionists, artists often disrupt our ways of seeing the world and provoke thought. A classic afternoon in Paris might involve visiting a contemporary art gallery, then retiring to a nice bar or cafe to discuss what you've seen. A great shrine to contemporary art is the Palais de Tokyo. Visitors find conceptual works of new and experimental media alongside more traditional mediums, like painting, photography and sculpture. The gallery stays open till midnight and hosts regular events to foster self-expression and discussion. It's a place for ideas; they're swapped at the bar, found in the library or bookshop and printed on the pages of the gallery's magazine. The Palais de Tokyo is a safe space for new perspectives to evolve as they pass through the hearts and minds of all those who visit.

DIY Engaging with contemporary art stimulates the mind and creates conversation. It's meant to be challenging. Visiting a contemporary art gallery is a great activity to do with a friend – just be sure to schedule in a debrief afterwards. Where can you see contemporary art in your city? Remember, contemporary art is not just 'art' as we know it – paintings and sculptures – but can be found on the streets and even the internet. Today, so much contemporary art can be seen online (films, games, digital artworks), so explore some of these platforms and challenge yourself to broaden your mind.

47

CUTTING
EDGE

CRÊPE STAND

48

Given the French passion for full-course meals, it can sometimes feel like the country is averse to snacking. Luckily, there are some street-side offerings to feed a peckish pedestrian on the run. Crêpes are wafer-thin pancakes, and they are ubiquitous on the streets of Paris. Vendors fashion crêpe batter into perfect circles atop heated griddles as the public watches (and smells) with delight. With an expert flick of the wrist, each crêpe is folded up and served sweet (with sugar and lemon, jam or chocolate) or savoury (with ham and cheese or an egg).

DIY Making crêpes at home is quite simple, even if shaping them into exact circles is not. Find and follow a classic recipe for Parisian, street-style crêpes (rather than the Bretonne version, which uses darker, nuttier buckwheat) and top to your liking. You can enjoy them as a delicious lunch or a light dinner. For a retro French dessert, douse your crêpes in Cointreau, butter and sugar, then light them on fire in your pan to make crêpes Suzette.

crêpes

For still and moving images alike, Paris has long served as the backdrop for visual stories (and it's been the protagonist of a few, too). Photographers have been captivated by the city's architecture, the forceful light and its many characters. Henri Cartier–Bresson took his compact 35mm camera to the streets, capturing people and happenings he came across. His ethos defined a new school of candid photography, elevating everyday people and life to high art. In the 1950s, Paris became home to a new school of filmmaking: the nouvelle vague, or French new wave. Auteurs like Franois Truffaut and Jean-Luc Godard took a similarly candid, everyday approach to Cartier-Bresson. Their films were made with small cameras, often with a loose, documentary feel, with stylistic hallmarks like jump cuts and fragmented narratives. Films of the French new wave might not be as easily digested as, say, a Hollywood romcom, but they shook the world of cinema and laid the groundwork for many film conventions we recognise today. Both photography and cinema are still well celebrated in Paris. There are boutique cinemas everywhere, and endless photography museums to be explored.

DIY It can be quite fun to take to the streets of your own town with a documentarian's eye. Head out with your camera (a smartphone is fine) and think of yourself as an outsider. Aim to tell the story of your neighbourhood on that particular day. Who are the characters and the animals, and what are they doing? What is the setting, what is the season, how does the light fall, and what makes the sounds you hear? The key is to notice everything. No subject is too mundane to be transformed by the camera. If video is your thing, experiment with recording your world and editing the footage to create interesting jump cuts or a non-linear narrative to tell your story.

49

CAPTURED
ON FILM

LOST IN THE WOODS

50

The Bois de Boulogne is Paris's own little forest at the west of the city. You'll find lakes and botanical gardens there, as well as a château, a zoo, an amusement park, a couple of horse-racing tracks and a stadium. The Fondation Louis Vuitton, with its soaring glass sails, was designed by Frank Gehry and is clearly the architectural highlight of the park. The woodlands of Bois de Boulogne were once reserved for hunting. Napoleon III became inspired after seeing Hyde Park in London and demanded the woodlands to the east and west of his own city be transformed into great parks for all. These days, Napoleon's vision has been fulfilled. People flock to Bois de Boulogne to go jogging and horse riding, have picnics, see music festivals, row along the lakes and even go camping.

DIY Museums *en plein air,* like the Fondation Louis Vuitton, are more common than ever. More and more contemporary galleries are opening in regional and rural areas. See what's available near your home town and plan a trip. Whether you're keen for the hike or the art, both work wonders for the body and mind.

Acknowledgements

Travelling to France from Australia, as I have throughout my life, is always a huge adventure – starting from the minute you kick off the gruelling 24-hour commute. Touching down to the flipped seasons and extreme jet lag, it's always clear that you're no longer at home, and your brain switches straight into holiday mode. The excitement of Paris is mostly due to the sheer fabulousness of that city – but the feeling of lightness and freedom, and having the time to do anything at will, shouldn't just come from travel. I have always wondered whether I could recreate at home my Paris-levels of enthusiasm for shop signs, cheese packaging and cakes in the windows. Now, I think I can. All it takes is a shift in thinking.

Naturally, the global pandemic turned our focus inwards. This upended our daydreams of foreign delights but also invited us to look around and see what we've already got – wherever we may be. Yes, there's nowhere quite like Paris. But I believe that working with (and learning to enjoy) what you have is one of the most important habits to cultivate in life.

A huge thank you to Mark Campbell for conceiving this book and helping me shape the myriad ways of bringing Paris home. You have taught me a few things about living creatively, and that's no mean feat in lockdown. Thank you to Mietta Yans for the wonderful book design, and to Patrick Boyle for reigning in my enthusiastic ramblings about Paris (especially the Food & Drink section) and making them clear and sensible.

Thank you to all my Francophile family – Mum, Dad, Lucy, Olivia, Jane and Ken – for teaching me the joys of France, and broadening my approach to living. While the natural chic of the French is not something I've managed to emulate (yet), the way they enjoy eating, drinking, art and the outdoors has shaped the person I am today. I'm grateful to all our friends in France who taught me *il faut en profiter* ('you must make the most of it'). It's an expression I remember whenever I have the opportunity to savour a few free hours, a sunny day or time with friends and family. If lockdowns have taught us anything, it's that making do with whatever we have – along with the odd daydream of Paris – can bring us joy from the simplest of things.

Harper *by* Design

An imprint of HarperCollins*Publishers*

HarperCollins*Publishers*
Australia • Brazil • Canada • France • Germany • Holland • Hungary
India • Italy • Japan • Mexico • New Zealand • Poland • Spain • Sweden
Switzerland • United Kingdom • United States of America

First published in Australia in 2022
by HarperCollins*Publishers* Australia Pty Limited
Level 13, 201 Elizabeth Street, Sydney NSW 2000
ABN 36 009 913 517
harpercollins.com.au

A catalogue record for this book is available from the National Library of Australia

ISBN 978 1 4607 6061 1

Publisher: Mark Campbell
Publishing Director: Brigitta Doyle
Editor: Patrick Boyle
Designer: Mietta Yans, HarperCollins Design Studio
Author and Illustrator: Alice Oehr
Printed and bound in China by RR Donnelley

9 7 6 5 4 3 2 1   22 23 24 25

Alice Oehr is an author, designer and illustrator from Melbourne. She spent much of her youth in France and can tell you everything you need to know about French supermarkets, the art of *l'aperitif* and navigating a French bakery. She was in Paris when Notre Dame burned and appreciates only too well the romance of the city. Writing this from an armchair in Australia, Paris still maintains its magnetism from over 16,000km away.